APA: The Easy Way!
Second Edition

Peggy M. Houghton, Ph.D.
Timothy J. Houghton, Ph.D.

Editor: Michele M. Pratt

Education is one of the best investments you will ever make…and our books maximize that investment!
Houghton & Houghton

Baker College
Flint, Michigan

www.houghtonandhoughton.com

For more information, contact:
Baker College Bookstore
bookstore@baker.edu
800-339-9879
Volume discounts are available through Baker College

Library of Congress Cataloging-in-Publication Data

Houghton, Peggy M.

APA— the easy way! / Peggy M. Houghton, Timothy J.
Houghton.

p. cm.

Includes bibliographical references.

ISBN 0-923568-96-2

1. Psychology—Authorship—Handbooks, manuals, etc.
I. Houghton, Timothy J., 1961- II. Title.

BF76.7.H68 2005

808'.06615—dc22

2008026401

Manufactured in the United States of America

Table of Contents

Preface

With more than 30 combined years of teaching experience, the authors of this handbook have learned that there has been considerable confusion with writing according to the American Psychological Association (APA) guidelines. Those who are familiar with APA format realize that many students are apprehensive and rather perplexed with this particular writing style.

Although APA writing style is designed for those who intend to publish, numerous colleges, universities, and secondary schools adhere to these stringent guidelines for student papers. Years of experience have proven there are consistent questions and misunderstandings regarding the style. Consequently, this document has been developed to expand and enhance the APA writing experience. There are some APA guidelines that are optional; therefore, the instructor should be consulted for final authority with regard to writing assignments.

The handbook is divided into three parts. Part one focuses on the mechanics of APA format as well as internal text citations; part two emphasizes the actual reference page entries; and part three provides a sample paper.

NOTE: Throughout this document, single-spacing has been utilized. This type of spacing is used to simply save space. In addition, names and reference citations given throughout may be fictitious.

Part One
Mechanics of APA

Utilizing Microsoft Word
(for applications prior to Microsoft Word 2007)

The following are specific instructions on how to set up a document for APA format using Microsoft Word.

Margins

All margins (top, bottom, and sides) should be set at a minimum of one inch. Microsoft Word allows the user to set the margin at a default of one inch. To do so, follow the guidelines below:

1. Under FILE, select PAGE SETUP.
2. Select MARGINS tab and type 1" at TOP, BOTTOM, LEFT, and RIGHT boxes. Click OK.

Margins

Alignment/Line Spacing

All documents following APA guidelines are required to be aligned left and double-spaced throughout the entire document. Be sure not to include additional spacing between paragraphs, headings, etc. To set the default, follow these guidelines:

1. Place the cursor at the start of the document, select FORMAT.
2. Under FORMAT, select PARAGRAPH.
3. Under PARAGRAPH, set ALIGNMENT to LEFT.
4. Under PARAGRAPH, set LINE SPACING to DOUBLE. Click OK.

Alignment/ Line spacing

Font Type and Size

The preferred font type is Times New Roman. Additionally, APA requires the font size to be 12 point.

Font type and size

This is an example of 12-point Times New Roman.

To set both the font size and style using Word, do the following:

Font type and size

1. Under FORMAT, select FONT.
2. Under FONT, select Times New Roman.
3. Under SIZE, select 12.

Paragraph Indentation

All papers typed in APA format require paragraphs to be indented one-half inch. This can easily be accomplished by striking TAB on the keyboard.

Paragraph indentation

To set tab to the one-half inch default, do the following:

1. Under FORMAT, select PARAGRAPH.
2. Under PARAGRAPH, select TABS.
3. Under TABS, set DEFAULT TAB STOPS at .5".

Hanging Indents

To set the hanging indent feature, do the following:

Hanging indents

1. Under FORMAT, select PARAGRAPH.
2. Under SPECIAL, choose HANGING. Click OK.

Johnson, L. R. (2005). *People who live in glass houses should not throw stones*. Chicago, IL: Alleman and Anderson Books.

Page Header

Beginning on the very first page (title page) and running continually throughout the APA document, a page header is utilized. The page header should appear one-half inch down from the top margin. It includes the running head flush left and the page number flush right. On the title page, the page header consists

Page header

of the words *Running head* (the *R* in *Running* is capitalized) followed by a colon and the title of the paper in all capital letters. Subsequent pages should *not* use the words *Running head:*. See the sample paper for an example. There is a maximum of 50 characters (including spaces) after the colon. If the title encompasses more than 50 characters, then only major words should be used. This can be accomplished using the HEADER AND FOOTER function.

1. Under VIEW, select HEADER AND FOOTER. The cursor will appear flush left in the header box.

2. Type Running head: TITLE OF YOUR PAPER.

NOTE: The *R* is uppercase; the *h* is lowercase. Also, the actual title of the paper should be in all uppercase letters.

3. Tab twice to move to the right aligned position.

4. Select the # icon in HEADER AND FOOTER box.

5. Select CLOSE.

6. Move the cursor to the end of the title page.

7. Click INSERT then BREAK.

8. Under SECTION, choose NEXT PAGE.

Page header

NOTE: At this point, a second page containing the same page header as the first page will appear (except the page number will be 2 instead of 1).

9. Under VIEW, select HEADER AND FOOTER. The cursor will appear flush left in the header box.

10. On the HEADER/FOOTER toolbar, click SAME AS PREVIOUS to break the connection with the previous header.

11. Delete the words *Running head:* and introductory space(s). Click CLOSE.

Utilizing Microsoft Word 2007

The following are specific instructions for setting up an APA document using Microsoft Word 2007.

Margins

All margins (top, bottom, and sides) should be set at a minimum of one inch. Microsoft Word allows the user to set the margin at a default of one inch. To do so, follow the guidelines below:

Margins

1. Select PAGE LAYOUT from the ribbon tabs.

2. Select the MARGINS icon from the PAGE SETUP drop down menu.

3. Click on NORMAL.

Alignment/Line Spacing

All documents following APA guidelines are required to be aligned left and double-spaced throughout the entire document. Be sure not to include additional spacing between paragraphs, headings, etc. To set the default, follow these guidelines:

Alignment/ Line spacing

1. Select HOME from the ribbon tabs.
2. Select the PARAGRAPH window (by clicking the icon to the right of the word *paragraph*).
3. Under ALIGNMENT, select LEFT.
4. Under LINE SPACING, select DOUBLE.
5. Under SPACING set both BEFORE and AFTER to 0 pt. or simply click *Don't add space between paragraphs of the same style.*
6. Click OK.

Font Type and Size

The preferred font type is Times New Roman. Additionally, APA requires the font size to be 12 point.

This is an example of 12-point Times New Roman.

Font type and size

1. Select HOME from the ribbon tabs.
2. Select the FONT window (by clicking the icon to the right of the word *Font*).
3. Select Times New Roman.
4. Select SIZE of 12. Click OK.

Paragraph Indentation

All papers typed in APA format require paragraphs to be indented one-half inch. This can easily be accomplished by striking TAB on the keyboard (cursor must be positioned at the top of the page).

Paragraph indentation

To set tab to the one-half inch default, do the following:

1. Select HOME from the ribbon tabs.
2. Select the PARAGRAPH window (by clicking the icon to the right of the word *paragraph*).
3. At INDENTATION, set LEFT to .5". Click OK.

Hanging Indents

To set the hanging indent feature, do the following:

1. Select HOME from the ribbon tabs.
2. Select the PARAGRAPH window (by clicking the icon to the right of the word *paragraph*), and select the INDENTS AND SPACING tab.
3. Under SPECIAL, choose HANGING. Under BY, select .5". Click OK.

Page Header

Beginning on the very first page (title page) and running continually throughout the APA document, a page header is utilized. The page header should appear one-half inch down from the top margin. It includes the running head flush left and the page number flush right. On the title page, the page header consists of the words *Running head* (the *R* in *Running* is capitalized) followed by a colon and the title of the paper in all capital letters. Subsequent pages should *not* use the words *Running head:*. See the sample paper for an example.There is a maximum of 50 characters (including spaces) after the colon. If the title encompasses more than 50 characters, then only major words should be used. This can be accomplished using the HEADER AND FOOTER function.

1. Select INSERT from the ribbon tabs.
2. Select HEADER.
3. Select EDIT HEADER.
4. Type Running head: TITLE OF YOUR PAPER.

NOTE: The *R* is uppercase; the *h* is lowercase. Also, the actual title of the paper should be in all uppercase letters.

5. Tab twice to move to the right aligned position.
6. Select PAGE NUMBER option in the ribbon tabs.
7. Select CURRENT POSITION.
8. Select PLAIN NUMBER. This will right-align the page number.

9. Select CLOSE HEADER AND FOOTER (located in the upper right-hand corner).

NOTE: Steps 10 through 15 show how to create a section break between the title page and second page in order to change the page header. Step 16 shows how to alter the page header on page two and subsequent pages.

10. Place your cursor at the end of the text on the title page.
11. Select PAGE LAYOUT from the ribbon tabs.
12. On the PAGE SETUP menu, click on BREAKS.
13. Under SECTION BREAKS, select NEXT PAGE.
14. Click into the page header on page 2.
15. Click on LINK TO PREVIOUS to de-select it.
16. Delete the words *Running head:* and introductory space(s) and click CLOSE HEADER AND FOOTER.

Page header

Levels of Headings

When a document requires the use of headings, the following five levels should be utilized (*Publication Manual of the American Psychological Association* (6th edition), 2010, pp. 62-63):

Levels of headings

Centered, Boldface, Uppercase and Lowercase Heading
(Level One)

Flush Left, Boldface, Uppercase and Lowercase Heading
(Level Two)

  Indented, boldface, lowercase paragraph heading ending with a period.
     (Level Three)

  Indented, boldface, italicized, lowercase paragraph heading ending with a period.
     (Level Four)

  Indented, italicized, lowercase paragraph heading ending with a period.
     (Level Five)

---

6 · *APA: The Easy Way!*

NOTE: In levels three, four, and five, capitalize only the first letter of the first word.

NOTE: In levels three, four, and five, the paragraph begins on the same line as the heading.

Title Page

The title page of the document should include the following:

- Page header: Running head is flush left; page number is flush right.

- Title of the paper, student's name, and name of college or university (centered on the page).

The Running head will appear .5" from the top of the page. The *R* is uppercase, while the *h* is lowercase. After the words *Running head,* there is a colon, one space, and the title of the paper typed in all uppercase letters. Note that this is the only part of the APA document that will appear in all uppercase lettering. Also, there is a limit of 50 maximum total characters starting after the colon…counting spaces. It may be necessary to use only main words of the title.

Title Page

Running head: MOTIVATING EMPLOYEES

The page header will appear one-half inch from the top margin on each page. At the left margin, the words *Running head* should appear, followed by a colon and the title of the paper (typed in all uppercase lettering). This title should be 50 characters maximum, including spaces. The page number should appear in the page header flush right. The *header* feature in Word should be utilized when establishing the page header.

The title of the paper, student's name, and name of college or university should be typed in that order and be centered on the title page (see Part Three for example).

Abstract

The word *Abstract* should be centered, one inch from the top of the page. The actual abstract, however, should be left justified. This is the only paragraph of the paper that is not indented.

Abstract

Abstract

It should be concise, accurate, and reflect the content of the document. The abstract should be only one paragraph in length. No paraphrasing or direct quotations should be included (see Part Three for example).

Appendices

Appendices

Appendices are pages at the end of the paper (after the references) with additional information. Appendices allow the author to include information that would be distracting to the reader if included in the body of the paper. Tables or charts more than a half page in length are often placed in the appendices rather than the text of the paper. The page header continues onto pages containing an appendix.

NOTE: If only one appendix is included, it should be labeled *Appendix* and centered, with uppercase and lowercase letters. If more than one appendix is included, they should be labeled *Appendix A, Appendix B*, etc.

Body of Paper

Body of Paper

Writers are strongly encouraged to develop the Reference page prior to in-text citations. This simplifies the process of writing the in-text citations, as these citations are derived from the actual reference page.

General APA Guidelines

- Italicize a word or words to reflect emphasis.

- The first line of every paragraph (other than the abstract) should be indented .5". If the TAB key defaults at .5", simply strike the TAB key.

- Generally speaking, avoid using the word *I*, unless you are the sole author of the document. Likewise, avoid using the word *we*, unless you are a co-author of the document.

- Person refers to the writer's viewpoint. First-person is the writer speaking; second-person is the person being spoken to; and third-person is the person being spoken about.

- First-person pronouns include the following: I, me, my, mine (singular); we, us, our, ours (plural).

- Second-person pronouns include the following: you, your, yours (singular and plural).

- Third-person pronouns include the following: he, she, it, him, her, his, hers (singular); they, them, their, theirs (plural).

In-text Citations

- Always provide appropriate credit; otherwise, it is considered plagiarism.

- Everything cited in the text must appear on the Reference page; likewise, everything cited on the Reference page must appear within the text.

- When paraphrasing an author, the punctuation (period) should be placed *after* the actual reference citation. For example:

In-text citations

> (Robbins, 2008).

Not

> . (Robbins, 2008)

- When citing a direct quotation less than 40 words, the punctuation (period) should be placed *after* the actual reference citation. For example:

> (Smith, 2005, p. 6).

Not

> . (Smith, 2005, p. 6)

- When citing a direct quotation 40 words or greater, the entire quotation is indented .5" and no quotation marks are required. The indentation implies that it is a direct quotation. For example:

> In their book *Between a Rock and a Hard Place* (1993), Roueche and Roueche include a memorable quotation from a developmental writing teacher just completing the first year of teaching in a downtown community college.
>
> I find it amazing that so many of my students will work so hard to make it when there is so little in their past to give them the confidence to try; I also find it remarkable that they finally achieve so much in spite of what at first appears to be overwhelming academic and personal odds; but what I find most unbelievable is that they take the chance and even come at all. (Roueche & Roueche, 1993, p. 121)

In-text citations

NOTE: When citing a direct quotation that is 40 words or greater, the punctuation (period) is placed *before* the actual reference citation.

- Use a variety of writing style techniques. Do not end every paragraph with the standard method of citing (author's last name, date published). This flexibility will allow for a more logical flow of reading. For example, use different techniques such as the following:

> According to Stemmer (2008)...

> or

> Stemmer (2008) indicated...

Consistent errors generally occur throughout citing in the text of the document. Although there is no specific order regarding the APA rules, the bulleted points below appear to be the most common errors found in student papers.

- *Paraphrasing an author*

Paraphrasing

When paraphrasing one author, provide the author's last name and the publication year. Note that the author's name and year are separated by a comma.

> (Tisdelle, 2008).

Additionally, the actual punctuation (period) is placed only after the citation...not before or before and after.

- *Order of multiple authors*

Multiple authors

When using a source with more than one author, always list the authors in the same order listed in the book or article.

- *Direct quotations*

There are two different types of direct quotations.

When stating a direct quotation (verbatim) that is less than 40 words, the entire quotation is placed in quotation marks. The actual reference citation should include the author's last name, the year published, and the page number where the quotation can be located.

There are a few things to consider at this point. The end quotation mark should appear at the end of the last word in the quotation. However, the punctuation (at the end of the quotation) is placed *after* the actual citation. In addition, the abbreviation for page is *p*. If using multiple pages, the abbreviation is *pp*.

Direct quotations

(Makel & Wilkerson, 2009, pp. 8-9).

Not

. (Makel & Wilkerson, 2009, pp. 8-9)

When citing a direct quotation that is 40 words or greater, the entire quotation is indented the same as a paragraph indentation and no quotation marks are required, as the indentation implies that it is a direct quotation. In this particular case, the punctuation (period) is placed *before* the actual citation, not after.

. (Dudley et al., 2009, p. 8)

Also, when a quotation that is 40 words or greater has a second paragraph, the second paragraph of the blocked quotation is indented further.

In their book titled, *Modern Day CEOs the Good the Bad and the Ugly* (2002), Heberling and Houghton noted the following:

In-text Citations (continued)

Direct quotations

> Throughout her troubled youth, Oprah would always have a refuge. She would turn to books as a safe haven. She was, and still is, an avid reader. Reading gave her hope and gave her the will to aspire to new goals. Oprah was exceptionally intelligent. Her strong intellect allowed her to skip both kindergarten and second grade. Oprah always praised her teachers for their guidance and support throughout her early years.
>
> Although Oprah lived with a myriad of people throughout her lifetime, she credits her grandmother for making her the success that she is today. This is primarily because her grandmother acted as the dominant support figure during her youth. It was her grandmother, and later her father, who were the ones who expected the best out of her; they expected her to excel with everything she did. Time would prove this to be an expectation that was ultimately conquered. (p. 196)

• *Secondary Sources*

When citing a source within a source, name the original work and give a citation for the secondary source. For example, if citing a paraphrased comment from Stemmer in Pratt's article

Secondary sources

(when Stemmer's original work was not read), reference the citation as follows:

Stemmer's work (as cited in Pratt, 2008).

NOTE: If a direct quotation was stated from Stemmer, the page number must also be included. Also, only Pratt's work is cited on the reference page.

Author, Date Citations

One author:

When paraphrasing one author, provide the author's last name and the publication year. Note that the author's name and year are separated by a comma.

Citing one author

(Karsten, 2008).

Two authors:

When citing two authors, use both authors' names every time, along with the symbol & when used inside parentheses.

Citing two authors

(Johnson & Klien, 2010).

Three, four, or five authors:

When citing three, four, or five authors, cite all authors in the first reference citation; in subsequent citations, use only the last name of the first author followed by the Latin term *et al.* For example:

[*first citation*]: (Bowen, Simpson, & Stewart, 2009).
[*subsequent citations*]: (Bowen et al., 2009).

Citing multiple authors

Note that there is a period only after *al.*

Six or more authors:

When citing work from six or more authors, always use only the last name of the first author followed by *et al.* For example, when citing work from Curtis, Jones, Brown, Johnson, Workman, and Smith, use the following:

(Curtis et al., 2008).

No author listed:

When citing work with no author, the first few words of the actual reference page entry should be used. Titles of books, periodicals, brochures and reports should be italicized, while titles of chapters, articles, and webpages should be noted in double quotation marks.

No author listed

Author, Date Citations (continued)

No author listed

> Some individuals believe that leadership is an innate skill that simply cannot be learned (*The mystery of leadership*, 2008).
>
> Leadership is not a scientific art ("Leadership versus management," 2008).

Anonymous author

Anonymous author:

When citing work where the author is listed as *Anonymous*, cite the term *Anonymous*.

> (Anonymous, 2008).

Authors with the same last name

Authors with the same last name:

When using different authors with the same last name, use the author's first initial within the text citation. This is the case even if the publication years differ.

> B. Robertson (2009) and T. Robertson (2006) extensively discuss leadership characteristics in Fortune 500 companies.

Multiple articles from the same author

Multiple articles from the same author:

When citing the same author with more than one publication within the same year, list the dates including *a, b, c,* etc. See page 23 for a Reference page example.

> Several published documents by Presnal (2008a, 2008b, 2008c, and 2008d)…

Personal communication

Personal communication:

When citing personal interviews, personal correspondence, or e-mail communications, state the interviewee's name followed by parentheses noting *personal communication* and the date on which the communication occurred. Use initials as well as the surname of the author.

> Talking with N. Macklin (personal communication, May 30, 2008)…

- Since this cannot be verified, no reference page entry is necessary.
- In subsequent in-text citations, use the last name and year of interview.

E-mail references:

> According to Paul Carey (personal communication, October 6, 2008), radio broadcasting is a challenging yet very rewarding career.

E-mail references

- Again, since e-mail communication cannot always be retrieved, no reference page entry is required.

Classical works:

> The Bible makes reference to accepting Christ as one's savior for eternal life.

Classical works

- Since portions of the bible are consistent in a variety of editions, no reference page entry is required.

Electronic references:

When no page number is provided with electronic sources, cite the paragraph number when paragraphs are numbered. However, the paragraph number is needed only in the case of a direct quotation. This can be accomplished by using the paragraph abbreviation *para*. In situations where the paragraph numbers are not provided, give the subtitle of the section along with the number of the paragraph within the section. If subtitle is too long to include, use a shortened title in quotation marks.

Electronic references

> (McDowell, 2008, para. 2).
> (McDowell, 2008, Union Power section, para. 2).

NOTE: All electronic references are cited in the same format as other citations. In other words, when paraphrasing, simply use the author's name and year published. If no author is provided, use the first few words of the title (italicized) and year published. When completed in this format, the reader can reference the actual reference page to get the specific webpage address and other citation information.

Tables

Generally speaking, tables and figures that enhance the content of the paper or manuscript can be included in the body of the text. However, if these tables and/or figures are lengthy or distracting, they should be placed in the appendices.

Within the text, tables should be referred to by number (see table 14). When explaining the table, only an overview of the respective material should be included.

Table 14

Adults in Red Run, SD, Possessing High School Diplomas

Age	Men		Women	
	Diploma	No Diploma	Diploma	No Diploma
2000				
20	13,312	11,413	18,345	9,288
21	14,429	10,006	21,317	7,215
22	15,087	9,436	23,113	6,793
Total	42,828	30,855	62,775	23,296
2010				
20	13,116	9,094	17,221	7,126
21	14,212	7,219	20,142	6,205
22	14,255	8,356	21,997	5,956
Total	41,588	24,669	59,360	19,287

Note. Adapted from "Education is on the Rise," by P. K. Roddy, 2008, *Journal of Social Commentary, 23,* p. 258. Copyright 2008 by The Social American Association.

Avoiding Plagiarism

Plagiarism is a growing problem in educational institutions both domestically and internationally. The word *plagiarize* is defined in *Merriam Webster's Collegiate Dictionary* (10th edition) as, "to steal and pass off (the ideas or words of another) as one's own" (1993, p. 888).

Plagiarism can take one of two forms: intentional or unintentional. When a writer knowingly uses other authors' works without providing appropriate reference citations, he or she is intentionally plagiarizing. If, on the other hand, a writer uses others' thoughts or ideas and does not realize that credit must be provided, he or she is guilty of unintentional plagiarism. Unfortunately, both types of mistakes can result in serious academic consequences. When plagiarism occurs, some institutions may require that the student receive a failing assignment grade; others may insist on a failing course grade; others may place the student on academic probation; and, in extreme cases, some institutions may actually expel the student.

It is incumbent on the writer to be forthright and honest with regard to using original and/or existing writing. Plagiarism can be easily avoided if the writer simply provides appropriate credit when borrowing ideas or citing directly from another individual's work.

When paraphrasing (rewording) work from another author, the writer must provide credit to the person who developed the original work. This simply acknowledges the fact that the paraphrased material was the work of another individual. It is not primary data (original); rather it is secondary data (information already in existence).

Likewise, when citing a direct quotation, appropriate credit must be given as well. Again, this signifies that the quotation is provided by another individual. When citing verbatim (using another person's exact wording), the borrowed material must be placed in quotation marks and properly cited.

Part Two
Reference Page

A list of references should be given on a separate page(s) at the end of an APA document. Every reference cited in the text should be listed on the reference page(s), and every reference listed on the reference page(s) should be cited in the text. However, note that secondary sources are not necessary as an entry on the reference page...only the original source.

References are a critical aspect of a paper since they allow readers to find and utilize sources cited in the text. References also indicate the vigilance of the writer, so a concerted effort should be made to pay attention to details (proper spelling, accurate information, punctuation, etc.). Most importantly, the reference section provides proper credit to authors for their work, which is why all information listed should be accurate and complete.

General 6th edition APA guidelines for the reference page(s) include:

In General

- Margins should be at least one inch all around (top, bottom, left and right).
- The page heading should be centered and called *References*.
- Double spacing should be used (examples used in this section are single spaced in order to save space).
- Bold type should be used in appropriate headings only.
- Underlining should not be used on the reference page.

Format

- Professional credentials should not be used on the reference page (i.e., Ph.D.).
- Personal conversations, e-mails, interviews, and letters should not be listed since the reader is unable to retrieve these types of sources (cite as *personal communication* in text, but do not list on the reference page).
- The first line of each reference entry should start at the left margin with the following lines being indented one half inch (hanging indent).
- Numerals are used to denote numbers ten and above.

Numerals
- References beginning with numerals should have the numeral spelled out.

"3 times the fun: The joy of triplets" should be listed as "Three times the fun: The joy of triplets"

- Acceptable abbreviations include:

ed.	Edition
2nd ed.	Second Edition
Ed.	Editor
Eds.	Editors
Rev. ed.	Revised Edition
Vol.	Volume (as in Vol. 1)
Vols.	Volumes (as in 3 Vols.)
p.	Page
pp.	Pages
No.	Number
n.d.	No Date

Abbre-viations

- State names should be abbreviated using the U.S. Postal Service two-letter abbreviations.

AK	Alaska
MI	Michigan
WV	West Virginia

- Spell out cities and countries outside of the United States.

London, England	Paris, France

- References should be listed in alphabetical order by authors (using surname of first author), associations (if the work is authored by an organization), and *Anonymous* (if work is signed *Anonymous*).

- Authors should be listed with last name first, followed by first and middle (if given) initials.

- If no author is provided, the title should be moved to before the date and alphabetized according to the first word of the title (excluding *a, an, the*).

Order of reference entries

When listing by author(s)

- First and middle initials only should be used (no complete first or middle names; one space between initials).

Comos, M. E. (2006) should be used for a 2006 article authored by Michael Eugene Comos

- For one author, list author before date.

Schreck, E. P. (2007). *Mistakes of supervising a culturally diverse workforce in the USDA*. Boston, MA: Corrigan Books.

- For two to seven authors, separate authors with commas and use an ampersand (&) before the last author's name, followed by the date.

Sienkiewicz, J. H., Scarcelli, T. A., & Alexandrowicz, M. P. (2006). *Great high school athletes transition into coaching roles*. Clawson, MI: Roddy Press.

Multiple authors

- For eight or more authors, separate the first six authors with commas, then use an ellipsis (three periods with a space before and after each) to connect the sixth author to the last author, followed by the date.

Multiple authors	Partz, M., Mentro, J. P., Harcelli, T., Banshi, P. P., Cretzell, G., Smith, C. E., . . . Sauls, C.E. (2008). A qualitative study of modern Native American dance. *Journal of Dance Methodology, 12*(3), 12-21.

- The publication date should be placed in parentheses after the author's name(s).

	Harcourt, J. (2008). The influence of peer pressure on dating within the same group of friends. *Journal of Social Interaction, 55*, 312-319.

NOTE: The entire date should be used when citing magazine articles, newspaper articles, or newsletters. In journal articles, it is necessary to use only the year, assuming that the issue number is provided. If page numbers are consecutive within a volume, no issue number is needed.

Publication dates

- Use *n.d.* after the author's name if no date is available.

	Zajciw, P. (n.d.). *Ukrainian culture in United States' elementary schools*. Miami, FL: Dolson Books.

- Use *in press* after the author's name if his or her work is in press (not yet published).

	Bojelay, M. J. (in press). *Beginning a successful career in real estate: Ten secrets you need to know.* Chicago, IL: Petersville.

- List publication dates chronologically (the earliest first) if an author has more than one reference entry cited.

Multiple citations by the same author	Ahern, J. (2005). *The beginning of electricity*. New York, NY: Lawrence House.
	Ahern, J. (2006). *Electricity as we know it today*. New York, NY: Lawrence House.
	Ahern, J. (2008). *Electricity in the future*. New York, NY: Lawrence House.

- Multiple citations containing the same author should list the single author first (regardless of date).

> Talbot, B. P. (2005). *Marketing retail cosmetics in California*. New York, NY: Mitch Clawson Press.
>
> Talbot, B. P., & Peace, J. (2004). *Packaging technology in the United Kingdom*. New York, NY: Mitch Clawson Press.

- Multiple citations containing the same author and different second or third authors should be listed alphabetically by the surname of the second author (or third author if the second author is the same).

> Jones, T., & Henson, R. I. (2006). *Fire prevention in schools*. Philadelphia, PA: Johannesburg Books.
>
> Jones, T., & Timocco, M. (2005). *Fire prevention at work*. Philadelphia, PA: Johannesburg Books.
>
> Jones, T., Timocco, M., & Smith, R. L. (2007). *Fire prevention at home*. Philadelphia, PA: Johannesburg Books.
>
> Jones, T., Timocco, M., & Yandley, P. T. (2003*). Fire: A historical analysis*. Philadelphia, PA: Johannesburg Books.

Multiple citations by the same author

- Multiple citations containing the same author and year should be listed alphabetically by the title of the book or article.
- A lowercase *a, b, c,* etc. should be used after the year to distinguish the entries. This is also used in the in-text citations.

> Munson, R. (2006a). *Human socialization at home*. Chicago, IL: Hawthorne Press.
>
> Munson, R. (2006b). *Human socialization at work*. Chicago, IL: Hawthorne Press.

Order of Reference Entries (continued)

When listing by association (if author is unknown, but not anonymous)

- The association should use upper and lowercase letters.

American Psychological Association
The Florida Guide to College Scholarships

Entries by association

- The publication date should be placed in parentheses after the association.

Patrick S. Houghton Heart Foundation. (2005).

- Use *n.d.* after the association if no date is available.

Warren Woods High School. (n.d.).

- Use *in press* after the association if the work is in press (not yet published).

Detroit Cancer Society. (in press).

Anonymous author

When listing by Anonymous (if signed Anonymous)

- The word *Anonymous* should be used if the work is signed Anonymous (alphabetize this as if *Anonymous* is a true name).

Anonymous. (2007).

When listing publishers

- Full names should be used for any university press or association acting as publisher.

Publisher entries

Wayne State University Press

- Unessential terms such as *Co.* or *Publishers* should be excluded, but terms such as *Press* or *Books* should be included.

Johnson Co. should be listed as Johnson
Hernden Books should be listed as Hernden Books

- The city and state should be listed for all United States cities (use United States Postal Service two-letter abbreviations).

> Springfield, IL: Hernden Books
>
> Los Angeles, CA: Preston
>
> Lenoir, NC: Rock Valley Press

Publisher entries

- The city, state, province, and country should be listed for non-United States publishers.

> Windsor, Ontario, Canada: Thompson Books
>
> Berlin, Germany: Mueller

- The state should not be repeated if it is included in the publishing name.

> Columbus: The Ohio State University Press

When listing page numbers

- The abbreviation *p.* (one page) or *pp.* (multiple pages) should be used for newspapers.

- These abbreviations should be used in book citations only when referencing a chapter or a section of a book.

Page numbers

> p. C1 should be used instead of C1 for a newspaper reference
>
> pp. 312-321 should be used for a chapter or section in a book

- Periodicals other than newspapers should use page numbers only.

> Johnson, R. (2004). Talk on the streets. *American Psychological Review, 87*(3), 521-529.

- All numbers (figures) should be listed for inclusive page numbers.

> 521-529 should be used instead of 521-9

Books

- In general, a book reference should list the author(s), publication date, title, edition (if other than first), and publishing information.

> Jackson, L. P. (2008). *The times are changing for urban developers* (2nd ed.). Boston, MA: Allester and Bacon.

- A book title should be italicized, and only the first letter and proper nouns should be capitalized (unless using a colon, period, question mark, or exclamation point; then the first letter after the punctuation should also be capitalized).

Book entries

> *Modern management gurus*
>
> *Racism at work: The war in Mississippi continues*
>
> *Forget the stress. Start living better today*
>
> *Never give in without a fight! The basics of negotiation*

- A book with no author or editor should list the title, the year, and then the publishing information.

> *Communication in the workplace.* (2005). Cambridge, NJ: Boston Books.

- An edited book should list *Ed.* or *Eds.* after the editor(s) names.

> Dewa, P., & Runkel, G. (Eds.). (2006). *Chess strategies made simple.* New York, NY: Davidson Books.

- A revised edition of a book should list *Rev. ed.* after the title.

> Williams, D. (2008). *Physical therapy and the aging athlete* (Rev. ed.). Detroit, MI: Wayne State University Press.

- A subsequent edition of a book should list the edition in parentheses after the title.

> Lapensee, D. L. (2010). *Financial incentives behind sibling rivalries in family business* (2nd ed.). Baltimore, MD: BBM College Press.

- In general, a book published by the author should list *Author* as the publisher.

Book entries

> American Psychological Association. (2010). *Publication manual of the American Psychological Association* (6th ed.). Washington, DC: Author.

- In general, a chapter in an edited book should list the author(s), publication date of book, chapter title, book editor(s), book title, pages, and publishing information.

> Shurlez, S. S. (2007). Rethinking manufacturing. In P. J. Samakal (Ed.), *Modern business strategies* (pp. 63-78). New York, NY: Pemberton Books.

- In general, an article in an edited book should list the author(s), publication date of book, article title, book editor(s), book title, pages, and publishing information.

> Czajkowski, A. (2006). Asian politics. In P. T. Homes (Ed.), *World politics today* (pp. 87-99). Ames, IA: Wiley Books.

Articles within books

- An article in a volume in a series should list the author(s), publication date of book, article title, series editor, volume editor, volume title, volume number, volume series, edition, pages, and publishing information.

> Cook, T. C. (2005). Meat inspection in pilot plants. In D. K. Wlasiuk (Series Ed.) & J. K. Grems (Vol. Ed.), *Meat inspection: Vol. 4. Small plant issues* (4th ed., pp. 27-34). Los Angeles, CA: Hillman.

Books (continued)

- An encyclopedia or dictionary should list the author(s) [if signed], publication date, subject title (if available), editor(s) (if given), book title, edition, volume(s), page(s), and publishing information.

> Ritter, J. R., & Wells, P. (2007). Physical strength. In J. R. Ritter, & P. Wells, *The British encyclopedia* (4th ed., pp. 25-37). London, England: Avonhurst Books.
>
> Mackson, P. D., & Erickson, T. I. (Eds.). (2005). *Johnson's dictionary of psychiatry* (5th ed., Vol. 2, pp. 652-375). Buffalo, NY: Massillon.
>
> Peters, V., & Henz, T. R. (2007). Fossil fuel. In *The new world encyclopedia* (Vol. 19, pp. 440-449). Yutan, NE: New World Encyclopedia.

Encyclopedias and dictionaries

- An encyclopedia with no author or editor should list the subject title, publication date, book title, edition (if given), volume, pages, and publishing information.

> Missouri. (2008). In *The encyclopedia of the Americas* (Vol. 21, pp. 210-218). Dripping Springs, TX: Encyclopedia of the Americas.

- A dictionary with no author or editor should list the book title, edition (if given), publication date, and publishing information.

> *Merriam-Webster's collegiate dictionary* (12th ed.). (2007). Springfield, MA: Merriam-Webster.

- A manual published by an association should list the association, year, book title, edition (if given), and publishing information.

- Use *Author* in the publisher position if the publisher is the same as the author.

> American Dental Association. (2007). *Diagnostic manual of gum disease* (6th ed.). Fort Wayne, IN: Author.

Journals

- In general, a journal reference should list the author(s), publication date, article title, journal title, volume, issue, and page numbers.

> Roddy, P. K. (2004). A study of communication between a 1964 rock band and youth: The influence of The Rolling Stones on American teenagers. *Journal of Social Commentary, 23*(2), 254-287.

- An article title should not be italicized or placed in quotation marks, and only the first letter and proper nouns should be capitalized (unless using a colon, period, question mark, or exclamation point; then the first letter after the punctuation should also be capitalized).

> Do employees really love their jobs? Studies indicate 'yes.'

- Journal titles should be italicized, using upper and lowercase letters (significant words should be capitalized).

> *Journal of Applied Physics*

NOTE: Only list page numbers…do not use *p.* or *pp.*

NOTE: The volume and issue number are required for journals. In the previous example, 23 = volume number while 2 = issue number. The volume number is italicized. The issue number is placed in parentheses, with no space or punctuation between the volume and issue.

Magazines

- In general, a magazine reference should list the author(s), entire publication date, article title, magazine title, volume, and page numbers.

> Hoban, D. M. (2007, July 23). Fighting high cholesterol in diabetic adults. *Healthweek, 12*(2), 54-57.

- Magazine titles should be italicized, using upper and lowercase letters (significant words should be capitalized).

> *Modern Investing*

Magazines

- An article title should not be italicized or placed in quotation marks, and only the first letter and proper nouns should be capitalized (unless using a colon, period, question mark, or exclamation point; then the first letter after the punctuation should also be capitalized).

> The market crash: Are we done yet?

NOTE: Only list numbers...do not use *p.* or *pp.*

NOTE: The volume number is required for magazines. In the previous example, 12 = volume number while 2 = issue number (optional). The volume number is italicized. The issue number, if available, is placed in parentheses, with no space or punctuation between the volume and issue.

Newspapers

- In general, a newspaper reference should list the author(s), entire publication date, article title, newspaper title, and pages (separate non-consecutive pages with a comma).

Helm, T. R. (2007, May 23). Terrorism in the food chain. *The Montgomery Times*, pp. A1, A11.

NOTE: Use *p.* or *pp.* before page numbers.

- An article with no author should list the article title, publication date, newspaper title, and pages (non-consecutive separated by commas).

Gambling: Who really loses? (2006, January 27). *The Shreveport Gazette*, pp. B5-B6, B12.

- A letter to the editor should list *[Letter to the editor]* after the title.

Yastremski, P. R. (2008, August 21). Olympics need stricter drug screening protocol [Letter to the editor]. *The Alabama Daily*, p. C2.

- Newspaper titles should be italicized, using upper and lowercase letters (significant words should be capitalized).

The Cincinnati Tribune

- An article title should not be italicized or placed in quotation marks, and only the first letter and proper nouns should be capitalized (unless using a colon, period, question mark, or exclamation point; then the first letter after the punctuation should also be capitalized).

Simpson wins primary by a landslide!

Reports

- In general, a report reference should list the author (or organization), publication date, report title, issue number (or report number), and publishing information.

United States Mental Health Service. (2008). *Statistical data for psychological research* (USMHS Publication No. 43). Washington, DC: U.S. Government Printing Office.

- A university report should list the name of the reporting department after the university name.

Kowlakowski, D., & Martz, D. (2007). *Eliminating mercury in fillings* (Report to the dean). Minneapolis, MN: Delta University Press, Dental Committee.

- A report published by the author should list *Author* as the publisher.

Harlem Music Institute. (2007). *Hip-hop in urban areas* (HMI Report No. 12). New York, NY: Author.

- A report title should be italicized, and only the first letter and proper nouns should be capitalized (unless using a colon, period, question mark, or exclamation point; then the first letter after the punctuation should also be capitalized).

Safety research comparisons for the Ford compact vehicles

Unpublished Contribution to a Symposium or Meeting

- An unpublished contribution to a symposium should list the author(s), date, title of unpublished contribution, chairperson, title of symposium (italicized) title of meeting, and location.

Randazzo, T., & Somerset, D. (2007, May). Progress in the development of an anti-microbial agent for inhibiting pathogenic bacteria. In F. W. Lauder (Chair), *Meat processing*. Symposium conducted at the meeting of the Midwestern States Meat Processors Association, Dayton, OH.

Meeting presentations

- An unpublished paper presented at a meeting should list the presenter(s), date, title of unpublished paper (italicized), title of meeting, and location.

Fenster, R. L. (2009, June). *Ronald Reagan: Great communicator or great manipulator?* Paper presented at the International Conference on Presidential Leadership, Gardena, CA.

Reviews

- In general, a review for a motion picture, video, or book should list the reviewer(s), date, title [the medium being reviewed, and author or producer], the source containing the review, volume, issue, and pages.

- For DVD, film, video, or similar media, list the year of release after the title of the work being reviewed.

Hemp, J. P. (2010). The reality of religion [Review of the motion picture *The passion,* produced by the American Religious Society, 2009]. *Visual Psychology, 51*(1), 312-317.

Marly, T. (2008). Fact or fiction [Review of the book *My life,* by M.K. Sheckles]. *Basic Science, 27*(3), 210-213.

Partley, B., & Bobson, T. R. (2008). Why the fuss [Review of the video *Straight talk,* produced by Cops for Kids, 2008]. *Video Review, 21*(2), 21-44.

Reviews

- A review for a motion picture, video, or book should have the title (of that being reviewed) italicized, and only the first letter and proper nouns should be capitalized (unless using a colon, period, question mark, or exclamation point; then the first letter after the punctuation should also be capitalized).

Understanding emotional intelligence

- The source containing the review should be italicized, using upper and lowercase letters (significant words should be capitalized).

Contemporary Psychology

Dissertations and Theses

- Master's theses and doctoral dissertations are available from personal websites, institutional archives, and databases.

- A doctoral dissertation obtained from a database published by UMI (University Microforms International) should list the author, publication date, title (*Doctoral dissertation* in parentheses), database, and accession or order number.

Carthworth, J. A. (2007). *The portrayal of young African American females in hip-hop music video* (Doctoral dissertation). Available from ProQuest Dissertations and Theses database. (UMI No. 80143267)

- An unpublished doctoral dissertation should list the author, publication date, title (*Unpublished doctoral dissertation* in parentheses), institution, and location.

Billesti, M. R. (2008). *The effects of aging on Asian population growth* (Unpublished doctoral dissertation). University of Michigan, Ann Arbor.

Unpublished Works from a University

- In general, an unpublished manuscript should list the author(s), publication date, title, *unpublished manuscript*, department, university, and location.

McCale, H. L., & Torrell, N. (2009). *A quantitative analysis of birth control usage.* Unpublished manuscript, Department of Sociology, Rhinehurst College, Albuquerque, NM.

Unpublished Works from a University (continued)

Unpublished works

- An unpublished manuscript title from a university should be italicized, and only the first letter and proper nouns should be capitalized (unless using a colon, period, question mark, or exclamation point; then the first letter after the punctuation should also be capitalized).

> *The decline of liberalism in America*

- An unpublished manuscript from a university should list the city and state (if not part of the university name).

> Baker College, Flint, MI
>
> Michigan State University, East Lansing

Electronic Media (non-Internet)
Motion Pictures

- In general, a motion picture should list the names of major contributors with their titles in parentheses, publication date, title [Motion picture], country, and studio.

> Roots, K. (Producer), & Dumars, J. (Director). (2008). *On the road with an NBA championship team* [Motion picture]. United States: Waver Pictures.

Motion pictures

- A motion picture title should be italicized, and only the first letter and proper nouns should be capitalized (unless using a colon, period, question mark, or exclamation point; then the first letter after the punctuation should also be capitalized).

> *On golden pond*

- A motion picture should list the country where the picture was made and the name of the studio.

> United States: United Artists

Television

- In general, a television broadcast should list the producer, publication date, title [Television broadcast], city, state, and station.

> Belechik, G. (Producer). (2007, September 1). *Scared to speak out* [Television broadcast]. New York, NY: WMTW.

- A television broadcast title should be italicized, and only the first letter and proper nouns should be capitalized (unless using a colon, period, question mark, or exclamation point; then the first letter after the punctuation should also be capitalized).

> *Living with my mother*

- A television broadcast should list the city, state, and the name of the studio.

> Detroit, MI: WNET

Television Series

- In general, a television series should list the producer, date, title [Television series], city, state, and station.

> Jackson, L. (Producer). (2005, July 17). *The human body* [Television series]. New York, NY: WMEP.

- In general, a specific television episode from a television series should list the writer(s) and director(s), publication date, episode title [Television series episode], series producer, series title, city, state, and station.

> Cantrell, C. (Writer), & Donato, C. (Director). (1979). Swimming with the big fish [Television series episode]. In T. Jones (Producer), *San Francisco Bay*. Los Angeles, CA: WMEW.

- A television episode title from a television series should not be italicized or placed in quotation marks, only the first letter and proper nouns should be capitalized (unless using a colon, period, question mark, or exclamation point; then the first letter after the punctuation should also be capitalized).

> The night we found each other

Television series

- A television series should be italicized, and only the first letter and proper nouns should be capitalized (unless using a colon, period, question mark, or exclamation point; then the first letter after the punctuation should also be capitalized).

> *One big happy family*

- A television series should list the city, state, and name of the studio.

> Detroit, MI: WNET

Music Recordings

- In general, a music recording should list the writer(s), date of copyright, song title, recording artist (if different from writer), album title [medium], city, state, label, and recording date of the version (if different from copyright date).

> Barries, D. (1956). Johnny move over [Recorded by Ted Barker]. On *Songs that rock* [CD]. Springfield, MO: Pezzy Records. (1987).

Music recordings

- A music recording song title should not be italicized or placed in quotation marks, and only the first letter and proper nouns should be capitalized (unless using a colon, period, question mark, or exclamation point; then the first letter after the punctuation should also be capitalized).

> One step closer to God

- A music recording album title should be italicized, and only the first letter and proper nouns should be capitalized (unless using a colon, period, question

mark, or exclamation point; then the first letter after the
punctuation should also be capitalized).

Kiss: Live at Tiger Stadium

- A music recording should list the city and state where the
  recording was made and the name of the label.

Pittsburgh, PA: SMD Records

Computer Software

- Computer software should list the author(s) or
  rightsholder(s), date, software title (name), version
  (if applicable), program (or software or manual – in
  brackets), city, state, and producer.

Parnello, J. (2008). Production output analyzer (Version 3) [Computer software]. Buffalo, NY: Spectra Systems.

- A software, program, or language title (name) should not
  be italicized or put in quotation marks, and only the first
  letter and proper nouns should be capitalized (unless using a
  colon, period, question mark, or exclamation point; then the
  first letter after the punctuation should also be capitalized).

Statistical software for marketing program development

- A software, program, or language source should list the
  city and name of the producing organization.

Springfield, IL: Vision Analytics

- Standard software such as Microsoft Word or Microsoft
  Excel does not need to be listed.

Electronic Media (Internet)

- Internet resources are often the most difficult to properly
  list since addresses change, move, or become unavailable.
- Be certain to accurately transcribe the entire address,
  using upper and lowercase letters exactly as they appear
  (copy and paste the address if possible).

Electronic Media (Internet) (continued)

Internet

- Retrieval date should not be listed unless the document referenced changes over time (such as medical research or legal statutes).

- If a Uniform Resource Locator (URL) needs to be divided between lines, attempt to do so after a slash and do not hyphenate.

- If the URL ends the entry, do not use a period at the end of the entry.

- Database information, such as ERIC, does not need to be included since coverage can change.

- If a document can only be located in a database and there is no DOI, list the URL of the database.

- A digital object identifier (DOI) should be used whenever available.

- List page numbers if available.

Internet Journals (and other periodicals)

- A journal article found on the Internet should list the author(s) or editor(s), publication date, article title, journal title, volume, issue, page numbers and digital object identifier (DOI) [if available].

Internet journals

Ostroff, C. (2002). The relationship between satisfaction, attitudes, and performance: An organizational level analysis. *Journal of Applied Psychology, 12*(2), 963-974. doi:10:2114-445.57.291

- A journal article with no DOI available should list the URL.

Griffeth, R.W., Hom, P. W., & Gaertner, S. (2004). A meta-analysis of antecedents and correlates of employee turnover. Update, moderator tests, and research implications for the next millennium. *Journal of Management, 26*(3), 463-476. Retrieved from http://www.nwlink.com/~donplark/leader/learnor2.html

- Journal titles should be italicized, using upper and lowercase letters (significant words should be capitalized).

> *Journal of Sociology*

- An article title should not be italicized or placed in quotation marks, and only the first letter and proper nouns should be capitalized (unless using a colon, period, question mark, or exclamation point; then the first letter after the punctuation should also be capitalized).

Internet journals

> A statistical analysis of employee turnover in retail

- A special issue of a journal should list [*Special issue*] after the article title.

> Spentz, J. A., & Marles, T. P. (Eds.). (2009). Gun control in Iraq [Special issue]. *International Review, 12*(2), 142-156. doi:10:9067.32.45.6628

Other Internet Documents (non-periodicals)

- In general, if no date is provided, *n.d.* should be utilized.

- A document with no author or date should list the title, (*n.d.*), and URL.

- Internet titles should be italicized, using upper and lowercase letters (significant words should be capitalized).

Internet documents

> *Hispanic men in the corporate world.* (n.d.). Retrieved from http://www.psychek.com/psy/edu.htm

- A document from an organization with no publication date should list the organization, (n.d.), title, and homepage URL.

> Healthy Living Foundation. (n.d.). *Living sugar free.* Retrieved from http://www.hlf.org

- A chapter or article of a book authored by an organization should list the organization, publication date, editor(s), chapter or article title (in italics), page numbers (in parentheses), and URL.

Other Internet Documents (continued)

> National Business Research Council. (2009). In T. L. Roils (Ed.), *Standards for conducting business* (pp. 91-107). Retrieved from http://www.nbrc.org/standards

Internet documents

- A document obtained from a university program or department should list the author(s), publication date, title, and URL.

> Johns, K., & Sims, P. T. (2007). *Social structures within political organizations*. Retrieved from http://www.mu.edu/publications/papers.html

Internet Technical Reports and Research

- A U.S. government report on an agency web site should list the agency, publication date, report title, report number (in parentheses), and URL.

Internet reports

> Federal Bureau of Investigation. (2008). *Overview of white-collar crime in the United States*. (FBI Publication No. 843-1165). Retrieved from http://www.fbi.doc.gov/bbi/trade.htm

- A report or research title should be italicized, and only the first letter and proper nouns should be capitalized (unless using a colon, period, question mark, or exclamation point; then the first letter after the punctuation should also be capitalized).

> *Psychology in interpersonal relationships: A qualitative analysis*

Internet Meetings and Symposia

- A paper presented at a virtual conference should list the author(s), date, title, conference, and URL.

Internet meetings

> Merrill, T. J. (2008). *Merrill communication climate report*. Paper presented at Merrill 2008 virtual conference. Retrieved from http://www.merrill.com/topicofthemonth/press.html

- A paper or abstract title from a meeting or symposium should be italicized, and only the first letter and proper nouns should be capitalized (unless using a colon, period, question mark, or exclamation point; then the first letter after the punctuation should also be capitalized).

Psychological impact studies

Online Newspaper Articles from the Internet

- An online daily newspaper article from the Internet should list the author(s), entire publication date, article title, newspaper title, and URL.

Hewlett, M. T. (2007, March 23). Education helps stop turnover. *Boston Herald*. Retrieved from http://www.bostonherald.com

- Newspaper titles should be italicized, using upper and lowercase letters (significant words should be capitalized).

The Seattle Times

- An article title should not be italicized or placed in quotation marks, and only the first letter and proper nouns should be capitalized (unless using a colon, period, question mark, or exclamation point; then the first letter after the punctuation should also be capitalized).

Urban sprawl affects classroom space

Online Newsletters from the Internet

- An article from a newsletter with no author should list the article title, publication date, newsletter title, and URL.

Robberies increase in south end of city. (2009, Fall). *Town Acres Newsletter*. Retrieved from http://www. townacres.org/fall9/headline.html

Online Newsletters from the Internet (continued)

- Newsletter titles should be italicized, using upper and lowercase letters (significant words should be capitalized).

Online newsletters

> *Harlan Happenings*

- An article title should not be italicized or placed in quotation marks, and only the first letter and proper nouns should be capitalized (unless using a colon, period, question mark, or exclamation point, then the first letter after the punctuation should also be capitalized).

> Residents form health committee: Money is main issue

Online Magazine/Journal Articles from the Internet

- An online magazine or journal article retrieved from the Internet should list the author(s), publication date, article title, journal title, volume, issue, pages, and URL.

> Henning, P., & Stein, J. (2007). A controlled study of aggression: Inside a federal prison. *Journal of Experimental Psychology, 41*(2), 102-116. Retrieved from http://www.expsych.com

Online magazine/ journal articles

- Magazine and journal titles should be italicized, using upper and lowercase letters (significant words should be capitalized).

> *Journal of Organizational Studies*

- An article title should not be italicized or placed in quotation marks, and only the first letter and proper nouns should be capitalized (unless using a colon, period, question mark, or exclamation point; then the first letter after the punctuation should also be capitalized).

> An analysis of workplace behavior in non-profit organizations

Online Dissertations and Theses from the Internet

- An online dissertation from an educational database should list the author, publication date, title (*Doctoral dissertation* in parentheses), and URL.

Richardson, B. J. (2007). *Situational factors affecting the demise of higher education in the United States* (Doctoral dissertation). Retrieved from http://www.montanalinkage.edu/ett/

- An online dissertation retrieved from the web should list the author, publication date, title, (*Doctoral dissertation* and institution in parentheses), and URL.

Mavernesky, T. I. (2009). *The impact of verbal aggressiveness on European immigrants attending inner city schools* (Doctoral dissertation, Vermont State University). Retrieved from http://www.dissform.vsu.edu/doc/ths/

- Dissertation titles should be italicized, and only the first letter and proper nouns should be capitalized (unless using a colon, period, question mark, or exclamation point, then the first letter after the punctuation should also be capitalized).

The influence of modern dance on Native American communication

Online Video from the Internet

- An online video podcast should list the primary contributors (with their contributions in parentheses), date of podcast, title (*Video podcast* in square brackets), and URL.

> Rankin, J. (Writer), & Howerston, P. W. (Director). (2008, July 17). *Nice guys finish last* [Video podcast]. Retrieved from http://www.randj.com/

- Podcast titles should be italicized, and only the first letter and proper nouns should be capitalized (unless using a colon, period, question mark, or exclamation point, then the first letter after the punctuation should also be capitalized).

> *The social influence of entertainment magazines*

Online U.S. Government Reports from GPO Access Databases

- An online U.S. government report should list the issuing agency, publication date, title, and URL.

> U.S. Council on Aging. (2007, June). *Aging baby boomers: Are we ready for their retirement?* Retrieved from http://www.access.gpo.gov/aging/index.html

- A report title should be italicized, and only the first letter and proper nouns should be capitalized (unless using a colon, period, question mark, or exclamation point; then the first letter after the punctuation should also be capitalized).

> *Government bonds: Investing with confidence*

Part Three

Sample Paper

The following excerpts from the book *Modern Day CEOs* by Michael F. Heberling and Peggy M. Houghton were reprinted with permission from the authors. Some changes have been made to the original document to adhere to the APA standards described in this handbook. Because only portions of the text have been retrieved, the reading is not verbatim from the actual book.

The paper should be double-spaced with one-inch margins, though it might not appear that way in this publication due to typesetting issues.

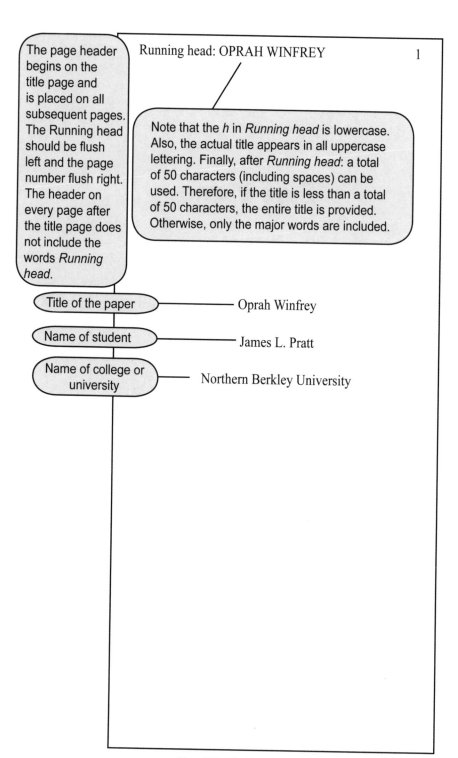

Running head: OPRAH WINFREY 1

The page header begins on the title page and is placed on all subsequent pages. The Running head should be flush left and the page number flush right. The header on every page after the title page does not include the words *Running head*.

Note that the *h* in *Running head* is lowercase. Also, the actual title appears in all uppercase lettering. Finally, after *Running head*: a total of 50 characters (including spaces) can be used. Therefore, if the title is less than a total of 50 characters, the entire title is provided. Otherwise, only the major words are included.

Title of the paper —————— Oprah Winfrey

Name of student —————— James L. Pratt

Name of college or university —————— Northern Berkley University

The header on every page after the title page no longer includes the words *Running head.*

Abstract

Oprah Winfrey is a world-renowned figure… basically a household name. The accomplishments earned throughout her lifetime are nothing less than stellar. Her die-hard followers and fans simply consider her a friend, someone they can relate with. They consider her to be a caring, loving, and compassionate individual. She had the conviction, desire, and ambition to overcome both childhood and professional obstacles that most would consider insurmountable. The chances of her succeeding in life were slim, to say the least. She not only beat the odds, she climbed to the top. Her celebrity status never reached her ego; and, to date, Oprah Winfrey is one of the most successful female entertainers/entrepreneurs in the world.

The word *Abstract* is centered on the page. The abstract is the only part of an APA document where the first paragraph is *not* indented. The abstract should be only one paragraph in length.

Title of paper ───────── Oprah Winfrey

Level One heading ─────── **Oprah...the Early Days**

Oprah Gail Winfrey was born January 29, 1954. Her name was actually *Orpah*, a name that came from the Bible's book of Ruth. Although her birth certificate reads Orpah, most people did not know how to pronounce it. People generally reversed two of the letters, thus creating the name *Oprah* (Brands, 1999).

Oprah's mother had multiple relationships throughout her lifetime. During some of these relationships, she would ask to have Oprah return to live with her. During one of her extended stays with her mother, Oprah's life would be scarred forever. When her mother left for work, Oprah was often left with an older male cousin. It was during one of these days, that her cousin would rape her. Oprah was told by the cousin never to say a word; if she were to say something, both of them would be in terrible trouble. Oprah agreed never to divulge anything. Unfortunately, this was not the only rape that would occur. Oprah was repeatedly raped in her own home by people who would visit her family. These terrible crimes resulted in Oprah possessing horribly low self-esteem...something that has had a deep effect on her till this day (Brands, 1999).

Brands (1999) further noted that throughout her troubled youth, Oprah would always have a refuge. She would turn to books as a safe haven. Reading gave her hope and gave her the will to aspire to new goals. Oprah was exceptionally intelligent. Her strong intellect allowed her to skip both kindergarten and second grade. Oprah always praised her teachers for their guidance and support throughout her early years (1999).

According to Brands (1999), although Oprah lived with a myriad of people throughout her lifetime, she credits her grandmother for making her the success that she is today. It was her grandmother, and later her father, who were the ones who expected the best out of her; they expected her to excel with everything she attempted. Time would prove this to be an expectation that was ultimately conquered (1999).

Adolescent Problems ——————————— (Level Two heading)

Oprah's academic success was not enough to prevent personal struggles. In an effort to gain attention and affection, she became sexually active. This ultimately resulted in a teenage pregnancy; the baby was born prematurely and died shortly thereafter. Oprah would eventually end up moving back with her father and stepmother. They expected Oprah to study endlessly and allowed her to watch television for only one hour a day...the local and national news (Raatma, 2001).

During her sophomore year at college, she was encouraged to apply for a position at WTVF, a CBS television station in Nashville. When it came time to audition, her strategy was to imitate her idol, Barbara Walters. The technique was a success, and she was offered the job (Raatma, 2001).

While in her senior year in college, Raatma (2001) noted that another position became available to Oprah. This job, a reporter and co-anchor for the evening news, would require her to move to Baltimore, Maryland. She decided to take the venture.

(Example of a sentence with the author near the beginning and the year published following.)

She had mixed reviews in her new position. Her critics said that she would sometimes mispronounce words because she preferred to report impromptu as opposed to following a script. Since the station had signed a long-term contract with Oprah, they felt that they would find a new position for her. In 1977, a new station manager approached Oprah with yet another

Italicize the title of television shows

proposition. He decided to start a talk show titled *People are Talking*. The format of the program would allow members of the audience to participate in the show. It would be hosted by two individuals...a male and female (Brands, 1999).

People are Talking would eventually beat *Donahue* in the Baltimore television ratings. The show was soon picked up in other cities across the United States. Oprah was becoming a well-known television personality (Brands, 1999).

Level One heading

Problems Associated with Success

Oprah was becoming a true icon of success professionally, but her personal life suffered. She had serious problems with relationships that evolved throughout the years. When she developed a seemingly strong relationship with a member of the opposite sex, she felt obsessed with being with the person at all times. Her insecurity and lack of self-confidence clearly was due to her childhood experiences. Gayle King, her best friend and now editor of *O, The Oprah Magazine*, was always by her side offering words of encouragement.

Italicize the title of a periodical

Level Two heading

A.M. Chicago

Oprah's newfound success was now receiving national recognition, and she was ready for a change. About that time, the general manager of *A.M. Chicago* had viewed one of Oprah's talk show tapes. Before long, Oprah was hired to be the new host of *A.M. Chicago*. Oprah's biggest challenge was the fact that *Donahue* was based in Chicago. The Chicago audience took an immediate liking to Oprah. So much so, that she eventually beat *Donahue* in ratings (Brands, 1999).

Level Three heading

Success comes quick. Within 12 weeks, *A. M. Chicago* had more viewers than *Donahue*. Seven months later, her show was extended to one hour. She interviewed well-known celebrities such as Tom Selleck; Sally Field; Paul McCartney; and her personal idol, Barbara Walters (Brands, 1999).

The producer of the show, Debbie DiMaio, explained Oprah's secret of success in the following manner:

> She's 100 percent the same off-camera as on. People like her because they can relate to her. She's got all the same problems – overweight, boyfriend troubles, she's been poor. So when people see her on television they can say, "That's my friend Oprah." (Raatma, 2001, p. 51)

40+ word direct quotation. Citation follows indented block quotation; end punctuation (period) appears before the citation.

Her forte, however, was interviewing the average person. She would get ordinary people to divulge their personal traumatic experiences. These conversations were almost therapeutic to Winfrey. In fact, it was during one of her ordinary interviews that she openly discussed her most horrifying personal experience… being molested by numerous relatives and friends. According to Brands (1999), she said

> I think it was on that day that, for the first time, I recognized that I was not to blame… It happened on the air, as so many things happen for me. It happened on the air in the middle of someone else's experience, and I thought I was going to have a breakdown on television. (p. 298)

40+ word direct quotation. Author's name and year appear at the beginning of the quotation; page number is at the end. Again, because the quotation is 40+ words, the punctuation (period) is placed before the citation.

The Food Battle

Fear of failure was Oprah's greatest downfall. One way in which to deal with her mounting stress was food. Eating gave her comfort. Oprah would binge diet and lose substantial weight. This would work temporarily; but as soon as the pressure began to mount again, the eating would start as well (Lowe, 1998).

Due to a lawsuit hearing, Oprah was forced to tape her show from Texas for a period of time. Oprah spent many hours defending her actions in the courtroom. During her stay, she actually gained 11 pounds. She noted, "I was strategizing with lawyers at night. I couldn't help but eat pie" (Lowe, 1998, p. 111).

Oprah's Empire

The Oprah Winfrey Show

Oprah Winfrey soon gained the reputation (and ratings) of being number one in the talk show business. She was able to sympathize and, quite literally, empathize with others in desperate need. She would recommend books for her guests and audiences to read. These books would soon become best sellers. Consequently, the publishing companies suddenly began knocking on her door. They deluged her with books to read, review, and, most importantly, potentially endorse on her television program.

The classroom. Having the urge to test her skills at teaching, Oprah and her fiancé, Stedman Graham, agreed to team-teach a course at the Northwestern University. Bill Dedman (1999) writes in his article titled *Professor Oprah: Preaching What She Practices* that Oprah described her success as coming from setting goals and from achieving them. She described the value of having an authentic leadership style that matched one's personality. Leaders must look inward, admit mistakes, and recognize their weaknesses (1999).

O, The Oprah Magazine. In 2000, Oprah attempted to conquer yet another goal. She took on the position as magazine founder and editorial director of *O, The Oprah Magazine*. The magazine is published monthly and encourages readers to make the most out of life. It offers celebrity interviews, articles about health and nutrition, self-help columns, and much more (Raatma, 2001).

As noted in Raatma (2001), Oprah described the magazine's purpose in the following manner:

> My hope is that this magazine will help you
> lead a more productive life, one in which you
> feel a sense of vitality, cooperation, harmony,
> balance and reverence within yourself and
> in your encounters. That doesn't mean living
> a life without frustration, anxieties and
> disappointments. It means understanding that
> your choices move you forward or hold you
> back. (p. 93)

After the first issue was ripped off the stands, Oprah still was not content with the magazine. Clemetson (2001) writes in her *Newsweek* article that Winfrey complained that the layouts were not lush enough and the writing was not smart enough. She ordered several re-shoots and revisions for the second edition. By the third issue, the editor in chief resigned. Oprah was able to secure a new editor who, like herself, is a perfectionist.

A day with Oprah. Oprah Winfrey is a dedicated, die-hard professional. People who worked for Oprah do so with extreme loyalty. They work long hours and put forth great sacrifice to keep up with Oprah's demands. One former producer noted the following, "People adore her. They give up their lives for her. People who work [at Harpo] get divorced, put off having kids, have no outside lives. Because everything, all your time and energy, is given to Oprah" (as cited in Raatma, 2001, p. 80).

Oprah attempts to bind all employees to strict, lifelong confidentiality agreements. She keeps a

Example of a secondary source citation.

keen eye on her personal ventures as well. In the past, she barred the press from the course she taught with Stedman Graham at Northwestern University's business school. Students who chose to talk to reporters could face disciplinary action from the school (Clemetson, 2001).

Example of a paragraph ending with author, date reference citation.

Down-to-earth diva... control freak... silly... caring... perfectionist... optimist. These are all words that accurately describe Oprah Winfrey. Clemetson (2001) describes a typical day with Oprah:

> It's Friday afternoon, and Oprah Winfrey is in an otherworldly state of calm. Her staff, however, is frantic. Nelson Mandela is about to arrive for a TV interview, and producers are rushing through set-checks, tightening security and prepping audience members. Behind the closed double doors to her Chicago office, Winfrey is plopped down in a cushiony armchair, a candle burning at her side, talking about the past year, when an assistant calls in a panic. Mr. Mandela is 30 minutes early, and Winfrey is still in her off-air gear–a baggy sweater and a well-worn pair of pants. "He'll just have to see me with no makeup on," says Winfrey, raking a hand through her unstyled hair. At least a little foundation and powder? The caller pleads. "Look," Winfrey replies before hanging up the phone, "he's seen a woman with no makeup on before." Her instincts are right. Mandela is charmed by the casual welcome.
>
> > Four days later, Winfrey is in perfectionist mode. Looking back at the December issue of her new magazine, *O*, she holds up the cover and winces. "Ooh, there's

Second (and subsequent) paragraph in a block direct quotation is indented further.

a mistake!" she says, pointing to the word "generosity," which she thinks should have bigger type. Annoyed with herself for not spotting it sooner, she grabs a stack of past issues and starts flipping. "Didn't like that." Flip. "Nope. Never got that right." Flip. Flip. Realizing that she's obsessing, she blows out a whoosh of breath and refocuses her energy on pages she likes. After several satisfied nods, she returns to the December issue and declares: "I love everything in this!" Then she turns a page, spots another imperceptible glitch and adds sheepishly: "Except this. We should have moved this." (pp. 43-44)

Use the abbreviation *pp.* when referring to more than one page

It is clear that, as Winfrey's assets continue to grow at exponential rates, micromanaging will not be a feasible option for the multimillionaire. She will simply have to give up some amount of control in some areas.

Oprah's ten commandments. Writers have dissected Oprah as an actress, an entertainer, a counselor, a business leader, and as a female success in a male-dominated world. Readers can gain some extremely valuable insight into her inner feelings from a set of 10 commandments that she says guide her success (Lowe, 1998, pp. 168-169). They include the following:

1. Don't live your life to please others.
2. Don't depend on forces outside of yourself to get ahead.
3. Seek harmony and compassion in your business and personal life.
4. Get rid of the back-stabbers—surround yourself only with people who will lift you higher.

5. Be nice.
6. Rid yourself of your addictions—whether they be food, alcohol, drugs, or behavior habits.
7. Surround yourself with people who are as smart or smarter than yourself.
8. If money is your motivation, forget it.
9. Never hand over your power to someone else.
10. Be persistent in pursuing your dreams.

Conclusion

Winfrey is a tireless businesswoman with endless energy. She is a philanthropist who has donated millions to various charities. She is also an actress, television producer, CEO, and educator with a personal fortune estimated in excess of $800 million. Oprah Winfrey was named one of the 100 Most Influential People of the 20th Century by *Time* magazine, and in 1998 received a Lifetime Achievement Award from the National Academy of Television Arts and Sciences (Academy of Achievement, 2006). There is no question about the fact that she is a leader – but the thing she is most proud of is the fact that the American people relate to her and consider her their good friend.

References

Academy of Achievement. (2006, May 6).

Oprah Winfrey. Retrieved from http://www. achievement.org/autodoc/page/win0bio-1

Brands, H. W. (1999). *Masters of enterprise.* New York, NY: Simon & Schuster.

Branham, C. (1998). *Profiles of great African Americans.* Lincolnwood, IL: Publications International.

Clemetson, L. (2001, January 8). Oprah on Oprah. *Newsweek, 137,* 38-44.

Dedman, B. (1999, October 10). Professor Oprah, preaching what she practices. *New York Times,* p. C1.

Landrum, G. (1997). *Profiles of Black success.* Amherst, NY: Prometheus Books.

Lowe, J. (1998). *Oprah Winfrey speaks: Insight from the world's most influential voice.* New York, NY: John Wiley & Sons.

Raatma, L. (2001). *Oprah Winfrey entertainer, producer, and businesswoman.* Chicago, IL: Ferguson.

The word *References* is centered on the page; no colon is necessary

Example of a website entry

Example of a book entry

Example of a magazine article entry

Example of a newspaper article entry

Index